Sajid Abdul

The book is for anyone who has ever felt stuck. Who has looked at the screen of their life and seen only frozen programs of doubt, fatigue and noise. It is a journey back to your core self the original software, before the world installed its updates. Take a breath, Turn the page. Your reboot starts now.

Connect with him on Instagram @sajiddd.__ for updates on his works

English Language
Reboot Life Control Alt Delete
Book by
Sajid Abdul
♦
Published in August 2025
By
SMS Publications
E-Mail : Publicationssms@gmail.com

♦
Cover Design
Mehrin Nisa
♦
Printed at
Repro India Ltd.

ISBN 978-93-3424-940-8

REBOOT LIFE

Control

Alt

Delete

A Poetic journey

Sajid Abdul

Acknowledgements

Dedicated to every heart that had the courage to reboot.

Special Thanks to my wife Shereen for your encouragement & support.

Foreword

"Written in impeccable style, Sajid Abdul's first book Face-off@ The Reunion was a riveting read on why school is the dreamscape the heart treasures forever. The sentences flow like a rippling river of priceless memories. This is the nostalgia that deserves countless reprints. One of the best books in my exclusive collection. Good writers feel before they think." Wishing him good luck for the second book.

Sir Frederick Wright

Introduction

After the overwhelming response to Face-off@ The Reunion, that travelled across borders and touched hearts from every corner of the globe—I return, humbled and inspired, with a new voice, a new rhythm, and a renewed sense of self.

Welcome to Reboot Life: Control Alt Delete—a collection born from challenge, clarity, and courage.

Life doesn't always follow a straight path—it crashes, pauses, restarts. And in that chaos, we find poetry.

Reboot Life: Control Alt Delete is not just a collection of poems. It is a soul's journal, crafted from lived moments that shaped my poetic journey through love, loss, nature, relationships, regrets, and renewal. Every verse breathes from real experiences of romance that blossomed, of respect that was earned or broken, of tragedies that left scars, and of seasons that taught silent lessons.

These poems capture the heartbeat of life in its rawest form its unpredictability, its beauty, its grief, and its grace. From fleeting occasions to forever farewells, from the calm of nature to the storm of memories, each poem is a fragment of a life lived deeply and felt fully.

This book is for anyone who has ever wanted to hit reset, find meaning in the mess, or simply pause to feel.

Welcome to a poetic Reboot of life

Where *Control* is reclaimed,

Alt is the perspective shift,

and *Delete* is the courage to let go.

While my first book explored nostalgia, relationships, and the emotional reckonings of reunions, this second volume takes a bold leap into transformation. These verses are not just words—they are keystrokes of survival, healing, and self-empowerment. Like the familiar command Control + Alt + Delete, this book invites you to pause, reset, and reclaim control when life spins out of sync.

Each poem in this collection is a prompt a reboot for the soul. Some will challenge you to confront unspoken emotions. Others will comfort you like a quiet sunrise after a long storm. Together, they offer a space to breathe, reflect, and start anew.

Praised for its honesty and emotional depth, my first book connected readers from Dubai to Delhi, United States to Cuttack. Reviewers called it "Well written. It relates quickly to our memories.", "The book is a blend of unadulterated fun and unalloyed nostalgia", and "A good read across all genres."

Now, I invite you in this journey again with courage in your heart, curiosity in your soul, and with the willingness to press reset when life calls for a new beginning. This is not just a poetry book. This is your moment to reboot life.

Table of Contents

The battle between the Mind and the Heart

The mind always differentiates
But the heart removes differences.

The mind is often selfish
The heart is always empathetic.

The mind is always confused
The heart is always open.

The mind draws boundaries
But the heart crosses them.

The mind overthinks
But the heart finds peace quickly.

The mind is always reserved
The heart is always free.

The mind fears a lot
But the heart is very courageous.

The mind hates a lot
But only the heart knows how to love.

The mind knows best to divide
But only the heart knows to unite.

The mind never forgets
But the heart loves to forgive.

The new Era

Times have changed,

And so have people, along with their looks.

It is a new-age revolution of the new genre,

To which everyone is completely hooked.

Never before in history was there a chance,

To see all in one glance in one book.

Thanks to those brilliant professional brains,

That gave us Insta, Whattsapp & Facebook.

Unbreakable bond

The love for you will never come to an end,
The beautiful moments that we had spent
The differences we had,
I still can’t comprehend,
I miss you so much it’s all I can say,
my lovely and dearest friend.

Forever with you

The journey of life is impossible without

you.

You share and care all the way through

You understand my feelings,

so I cherish you.

We live only once, this is absolutely true.

I promise that I will be always be with you.

Cricket's greatest rivalry

They create history whenever they clash,
Crowds go berserk as dollars fly and flash.
They bat and bowl with grace so high,
With nerves of steel, they aim for the sky.
And never once they dare to miss a single catch,
Such is the thrill of an India-Pakistan cricket match.

Holi with Love

I can't be there on this special day,
so I am sending my wishes your way.
Thinking of you all, with joy that lasts ever,
Color your life with happiness forever.
"Pink, orange, blue, red or green,
The color of love is forever evergreen.

The Honor of a Mother

The best creation of God in this world is
Mother.
She knows no barriers and never does
she bother.
She goes wild if something happens to
us rather.
The love she showers on us cannot be
given by any other.
She loves us the most, more than our
dear Father.
Paradise lies beneath her feet,
Such is the honor of our Mother.

Let’s make their day

It's indeed a great honor for me to say,
Parents are the greatest source of
inspiration today.
They brought us up with love & care,
despite all odds in their way.
It's a blessing in disguise to have them
with us today.
It's our duty to take care for them, as
they need us every moment, every day.
Friends, let's take some time to wish
them on their Birthday.

The Prankster's Delight

It's time to have fun,

It's time to be cool.

Leave no stone unturned,

And make him or her a fool.

Rack your brains and try,

Some old pranks of school,

Make your friends go crazy,

By surprising them with an April fool.......!

Blessed with Innocence

Thank you, God
For the children of mine.
Who teach me things,
That blow my mind.
They entertain me
In the funniest way.
The innocence they possess
I wish it never goes away.

Save Every Girl child

I am created by God in a water world,
Where I love to swim and play.
But my happiness is always short-lived,
As I have to leave and go away.
I reach out to a different land
Where people stare at me in a very
different way.
I feel bad sometimes,
Wondering "Where I was, and where I am
today."
All I need is a little care and love
To encourage me to smile forever and stay.
I serve humanity round the clock,
And sadly, there is no end to my day.
I am a darling daughter, an adorable sister,

A lovable wife, and a caring mother, right

away.

Please don't kill me before my death,

As your dreams are mine as well

That's all I have to say.

"Save me from the wrath of the cruel world

And don't leave my hands halfway."

"Save every Girl Child in this world

Is my only request to you, God

Which I always love to pray."

The Changing Tide

In good times, everything glitters.
Even strangers become friends.
In bad times, you get shocks and jitters.
The same friends become strangers again.

The Price of Alcohol

It starts with a peg, then a pint
And soon it becomes larger than life.
The world calls it a status symbol
Of the glittering night-life.

Where you lose your senses,
Dignity and self-pride.
No religion of this world
Encourages having it by your side.
As time passes by,
It becomes dearer than life.

When someone asks you to stop,
It becomes a strife.
Finally, the attitude takes over
Like an uncontrolled wild life.
Suddenly it back stabs you
With a piercing knife.

You fall flat on the ground
And drift into an afterlife.
Therefore it's high time to say
No to alcohol and yes to life.

The True bond of Friendship

Father, Mother, Brother, Sister
All are ready made,
But it's a friend whom
We prefer first and do not hesitate,
we choose them for mere time pass
Despite too many mistakes.
But we still rely on them,
Even if they're totally fake.
Such is the love and bond of friendship
And the friends that we make.
Love your friend's, don't break their hearts
At least for God's sake.

The Essence of Love & Hate

I Love simplicity, hate hypocrisy.

I Love gratitude, hate attitude.

I Love solitude, hate multitude.

I Love honesty, hate duplicity.

I Love kindness, hate harshness.

I Love sympathy, hate animosity.

People love to live,

some live just to love.

But only a few hate to love,

as they always love to hate!

The Changing Seasons

Every season has its special beauty,
Be it summer, winter, Rain or autumn.
They change our lives with their presence,
As they come one by one.

Winter and rain are the best of all,
As its perfect time for great fun,
it's the real time to enjoy, roam
Explore the earth and bask in the sun.

The next is autumn,
Which is loved and cherished by some.
The most common of all is summer,
As it emerges with the scorching sun.

Sometimes, the heat becomes unbearable,

And reminds us of our grandmother's

warmth.

Seasons always gives us a fresh lease of

life,

Every time they come.

Marriage a Delicate bond

Marriage is a flower,
Filled with beautiful fragrance.
It is like a small needle,
That must be handled with intelligence.
It is very joyful and sweet,
If nurtured with care and embraced with endurance.

Yet it can also be bitter,
If one loses patience.
It can take you for a long ride,
If you have perseverance,
It can be handled perfectly,
Without any interference.

It just happens once in life,

If blended with perfect love and

benevolence.

Marriage is all about love,

Compromise, respect and dependence.

3 vital things you can't recover in Life

"The moment," after it passes by and is missed.

"The word," after it is uttered and said.

"The time," which flies away after it's wasted.

Therefore, cherish the moment available to you at any point in time.

Think before you utter something, for it could make or break a relationship.

Value time, for it is the most precious thing that flies away and never comes back.

Living outside the Norm

People do different things,

But I do things differently.

People love to have affection,

But I love to have distraction.

People love to share their feelings,

But I love to share sorrows.

People love to make more friends,

But I am happy with my enemies.

People love to joke on others,

But I love to show respect instead.

Nature's balance

Everything is paired in this world.
A clap consists of two hands,
a coin has two sides,
a shadow has two images,
the sun has two directions,
an ambition has two outcomes failure
or success,
a relationship is always two sided.
Then why defy nature and live single.

The Journey of Right and Wrong

There are two ways of leading a life,
One is wrong, and the other is right.
Wrong always begins with glamour,
Glitter, glory and ends like a dark night.
Whereas right always starts with grief,
Sorrow, pain and is like a helpless kite.
But in the end, right takes a big leap,
Towards success, happiness, joy and
delight.
Therefore, always think twice before you
decide,
To be wrong or to be right.
"This is my New Year resolution,
A small piece of advice to guide your
flight."

The Rock of Friendship

It feels good, pleasant and fine,

But some old memories

Still haunt me sometimes.

The people are the same

As when I moved

Ahead with time.

But only a few have learned

To live and refined.

However, a true friend is like a rock

Of Gibraltar at any crucial point of time.

Chase your dreams

If the goal in life is set high,
there's no need to panic or cry,
all we need is sincere effort to try,
despite all odds, one can surely touch
the sky.

The Colors of Life

The essence of flowers
Cannot stop from reaching others,
it's difficult for me to dream
Of a life without colors.
Colors paint the world so bright,
Filling our hearts with pure delight.
The red of love, the blue of peace,
In their shadows, our troubles cease.
The yellow sun brings hope and cheer,
While green brings calm and draws us near.
Every color hold a key,
Unlocking the soul, setting us free.

A Guiding presence

Someone is always with me
wherever I walk,
Someone is always correcting me
whenever I talk,
Someone is always guiding me in my
deep thought,
Someone is always telling me what to
do and not,
Someone is always caring and
loving, at times a lot,
Someone is always with me, I feel,
even if I am lost.

The Guiding Lights

It's difficult to love someone,
And it's easy to hate.
It's bad to curse someone else
For my unlucky fate.
But Teachers are the ones
Who showed us the path straight,
Teachers are meant to be loved,
For they are really great!

The Longing Gaze

Millions of dreams
Intact in my eyes,
the willingness of guts
To touch the skies,
a lonely soul, far away
From the din and bustle cries,
Behold that memorable moment
Of time that flies,
all I wish is one look of her
Once, twice or thrice.

A Month of Blessings.

It comes once in every year,
People bow with conviction and fear.
They eat less and shed more tears,
They worship day & night to get more near.

The entire month is so blessed that people pray,
They abstain from all sins and prefer to stay away.
Men, women, children of all age stand in unison and say,
Such is the beauty of fasting, which binds them together to stay.

Whispers of Nostalgia

Lot of books,

Less to remember,

Hours of classes,

Dreams of December.

Plenty of rain

In the month of September,

The friends I miss now,

Do you remember?

Echoes of the past

Gone are the days,
Which will never come again.
Memories of happiness,
Drops of rain.
Friends and foes in
Numbers and domain,
Sins and acts of love,
Sorrow and pain.
No matter how hard we try,
But all in vain,
Moments of past
Will never come again.

In Awe of You

You are strong,

Beautiful, and compassionate.

You are dynamic

And will always remain my favorite.

You are a true legend

In whatever you demonstrate.

I would love to see you back in action,

If you ever wish to affiliate.

Always by your side

My love never dies for you,

My soul always cries for you.

My time always flies with you,

My tears always smiles with you.

I always need you to hold me,

To walk all the miles with you.

Be with me always!

Anger: The biggest enemy of Mankind

Let's see what we gain and loose in anger.

Gain & Loss

G-Anxiety & L-Patience

G-Restlessness & L-Peace of mind

G-Haste & L-Ability to take right decisions

G-Hatred, & L-Love

G-Enemies, & L-Friends

G-Strength, & L-Vision

G-Rashness, & L-Calmness

G-Impudent, & L-Kindness

Ode to a Masterful Teacher

The language and literature
Which he imparted is indeed a treasure.
He is a mastermind of the subject
And I say this with utmost pleasure.
His style of teaching is so unique
That we just cannot forget it ever.
Those beautiful phrases and idioms
Still dwells in our minds forever.

Reflections on human nature

Someone who's always a friend

Cannot be an enemy.

Someone who truly believes in God

Cannot be an atheist.

Someone who's a real winner

Cannot ever loose in life.

Someone who believes in love

Can never hate anyone.

Embracing each new dawn

Every new day is another chance to
change your life.
Every new sunshine brings a ray of
hope to thrive.
Every day sets new goals and desires
to strive.
Every passing day has in it a long lost
and found love like life.

Eternal Friendship

Friends remain friends,
Come what may ever.
You cannot forget them,
Be it whomsoever.
Little and minor differences
Can break them never.
Once a true friend
Remains close forever.

Monsoon's Joyful Return

Welcome Monsoon with plenty of
drops,
Shower the entire world as everyone
rocks.
You brought back happiness for all
once again,
Millions of drops and drops in the
form of rain.
Tears of all have gone the moment
you came alive,
We missed you a lot and love to see
you back in life.

Time's transformations

Everything has changed with time.
Thorny bushes have converted into a
lovely shrine.
It reminds me of few acquaintances and
great friends of mine.
Moments of love, hate and war on
Valentine.
The old oak tree stands bare, its branches
now entwined,
Yet beneath its shade, our laughter once
aligned.
Old photographs faded, but the memories
are enshrined.
In the heart's quiet chambers, where they
are forever confined.

Time the most valuable thing

Time knows neither future nor past,

Time moves swiftly, ever steadfast.

Time breaks all emotions,

Time makes new relations.

Time is always on the run,

Time brings loads of fun.

Time appears but once in a fleeting while,

Departing often with wistful smile.

Time is the intricate game of the creator,

Time is the most magnificent initiator.

Nostalgic days

The school bell at morning still lingers
in my mind,
Morning assembly crowds of a
different kind.
The curiosity to meet the best
friends daily, cannot be redefined.
The final call of the lovely day and
the faint memories are now left behind.
Those lovely games played with friends in
days unconfined,
a life we all miss today is so difficult
and hard to find.

Difference between a School life and a College life

School and College

Rules / No rules

Discipline / No barriers

Quality Education / Boring lectures

True friends/ Mean friends

Teachers are well-respected / Lecturers are abused

Enough time to spend with all / Limited time

Fear of God and parents / No fear, no repentance

Independence within limits / No limits

Non-violence / Full violence

Mandatory / Voluntary

Unforgettable / Best forgotten with time

Butterflies & bitter gourd

Time comes like a butterfly
And goes away in the sky.
The more I hold it tightly,
The faster it goes by.
Happiness is always short- lived,
I really do not know why!
Every day presents a challenge,
So there's need not cry.
Face the world as it is
And never give up or be shy.
Life is full of surprises,
So don't be eager to bid it goodbye.
At times, it's a bitter gourd,
But then it turns into an apple pie.
Life is an unusual mystery,
Would you like to give it another try?

A special Bond!

It comes just once a year
A Sister never forgets at all.
All the blood relations pale
Before this special call.
It's a small piece of string,
Creating an everlasting impact on all.
Wherein the brother swears to
Protect his Sister's honor above all.
This is a special bond of love,
That always shines and stands tall.

A Tribute

It’s truly delightful

To see them all in one frame.

Friends, can we exert a little effort

To recall their names.

They epitomize beautiful teachers,

Who always joined us in our games?

They are all my Favorites,

And I’m amazed to see

That they still look the same.

A Special Birthday cheer

It's time to celebrate for our special friend,
let’s pester him a bit today and continue
this trend.
It's hard to believe his age,
He still looks cute and young at every stage,
so, friends, no matter he is far away,
let's wish him today,
A very happy Birthday and a very joyful day!

Strengthening our bonds

It's always a pleasure to find,
People who join our group are
warm and kind.
Let’s do our best to
strengthen our bond,
and share our love,
emotions and thoughts beyond.

Together we laugh, together we grow,
Spreading joy wherever we go.
Through highs and lows, we stand as one,
With Friendship shining like the rising sun.

Life a test of Contrasts

Good and bad,

Happiness and sorrow,

Right and wrong,

Defeat and victory,

Charity and crime,

Love and Hatred,

Honest and Crooked,

Brave and coward,

Clever and foolish,

Friend and enemy,

Generous and stingy,

Inferior and superior,

Justice and injustice,

Knowledge and Ignorance,

Loyal and Betrayal,

Obedient and Defiance,

Rich and poor.

Real and fake.

Believer or Atheist.

We live once, and we die once, no
second chances.

Heaven at their feet

The world is so beautiful
With countless amazing places.
People of different castes,
Colors, creeds and races.
But one place stands above them all,
A truth that time embraces
At the feet of our parents,
Where true heaven traces.

A Tribute to the Martyrs

Let's pray for the martyrs,
Who shed their blood for us to see this day,
they fought through endless nights
and days,
So we could cherish this moment and stay,
my heart is filled with joy and pride,
As I feel the urge to pray,
it's indeed an honor and pride, for us to
complete years of freedom today,
I love India with all my heart, wishing
you all a very Happy Independence Day!

The Power of Words

Words are not seeds to be sown around,
They are delicate once uttered, never
found.
Words can cause havoc, bring nations
down.
Easy for some, yet heavy for a crown,
So be careful with them, don't play around.

A New Year's message

The time has come for frolic and fun.
The moment to rejoice with everyone.
Celebrate with kith, kin and your special one,
Forget the past, embrace the rising sun.
May God bless our lives with happiness, cheer and fun.
This is my message for the year to come.

Cherished School Memories

Memories of the past will never grow old,
No matter they are gone, but few stories remain untold.
It's time to unwrap and let them unfold,
School Friends are Treasures, more precious than any diamond or gold.

A Guiding Light

It was difficult for me
To learn all good things overnight.
Mom taught me step by step,
Guiding me with patience, day and night.
Dad always taught me
How to be a winner in every fight.
But the one who showed me
What is wrong and what is right,
It's my Teacher.
Who guided me always like a lamplight?
He came into my life as a blessing
In disguise with all his might.
He gave me new hope,
Like a beam of sunlight.
He is a friend, a tutor, a guide
He always shows the perfect light.

The Silver Lining in Currency

In the dark world of currency,
Came a silver lining of hope and light.
It promised bigger dreams,
And sought to change things overnight.
The bulls ran wild on the streets,
Only to succumb to the monstrous fight,
It took far longer than projected,
To prove if it was wrong or right.
People struggled, living hand to mouth,
As everything turned tight.
In the mission of glory, to our surprise,
The white shone brighter,
And the black faded into white.

Caution

Never believe all that you hear.

Never assume things that are not clear.

Never take anyone for granted out of fear.

Never trust until the truth is transparent

and near.

The Journey of Life

Life is not as easy as it appears.
The sun rises in the east
And in the west it disappears.
Childhood came and went by
In the blink of an eye.
The best thing it left behind
Is few sweet memories of fun with friends
of mine.
Life is full of ups and downs
Which will always scare you forever.
No matter how difficult the path may be,
You have to tread the path with your
friends together.

A Memorable Valentine

It's one of the best moments of a lifetime.

I was young, and so was love, a bit clandestine.

The first feeling of real love was of a different kind.

I was lost in another world, and so was my insane mind.

She walked silently into my life, and I was spellbind.

The nights grew longer, and days were left behind.

Her presence so enchanting, it blew my mind.

Love is so simple, but few ponder too much and fail to find.

It's the best thing to happen in one's life,

It's a real boon to mankind.

Wish you all happiness & love forever,

And a very memorable Valentine.

Special Moments

Some moments are truly special,

As they make our day.

Some people are unforgettable,

As we still miss them today.

Some days will always be remembered,

As they don't come every day.

Some lovely teaching will always dwell,

In our minds, forever, along the way.

Friends forever

Friends are still friends, come what may,
You cannot forget them, no matter what
they say.
Little differences can never break the bond.
A true friend stays close, always and
beyond.

Nature’s revenge

What's changed so suddenly?
That you all are away?

“We feel more fresh and vibrant”
Without you today.

You created too much noise
And exhaled venom every day.

“Our peace was shattered”
“Polluted by you in every way”.

We lost our elegance, our beauty,
And our fragrance day by day.

We love this new feeling now,
Since you’re no longer here to play.

We warned you umpteen times,
But you never cared, we must say.

We hope you’ve finally learned a lesson,
“That, ‘Every dog has its day."

Deadly Pandemic

I see no day, I see no night.

I see no black, I see no white.

I see no rich, I see no poor.

I see no time, I am always on tour.

I see no young, I see no old.

I see no border that can take hold.

I see you all fight, I see you all hate.

I see you blame each other, but I will not discriminate.

I see no caste, no creed, and no race.

I will continue to spread further, until you all unite and awake.

Differences between Love and Like

In front of the person you love, your heart beats faster

But in front of the person you like, you feel happy.

In front of the person you love, winter feels like spring

But in front of the person you like, winter is just a beautiful winter.

If you look into the eyes of the one you love, you blush

But if you look into the eyes of the one you like, you smile.

In front of the person you love, you can't say everything on your mind

But in front of the person you like, you can.

In front of the person you love, you tend to get shy

But in front of the person you like, you can show yourself.

The person you love comes into your mind every two minutes.

You can't look straight into the eyes of the one you love,

But you can always smile into the eyes of the one you like.

When the one you love is crying, you cry with them

But when the one you like is crying, you end up comforting.

Euphoria

The day went longer until one realized it
became night,

The sky glittered with various colorful
sights.

The excitement and the enthusiasm
never ceased, till the last fight.

The only thing that matters is to hold the
thread so tight.

The race to topple each other is always
crazy, with full might.

This is the euphoria and the passion of
flying a kite.

The Gift of Fatherhood

The mobile rang at six that day,
But deep in slumber, I chose to stay.
A hectic night at the hospital's door,
My wife in need, our spirits sore.

The doctor said, "Rest until dawn,
Nothing urgent till morning's yawn."
Though torn inside, I chose to leave,
My parents stayed, my heart on sleeve.

At home, I lay with anxious heart,
Fatherhood's journey just to start.
At seven-fifteen, the mobile's call,
Awoke me sharp that was all.

I jumped, I ran, the car sped fast,
Through the empty streets at last.
In fifteen minutes, reached the gate,
Fate had chosen not to wait.

Up the stairs, I rushed with fear,
Parents stood something unclear.
I peered inside, but couldn't see,
What lay beyond for wife and me
The door creaked open then I heard,
A baby's cry, the sweetest word.
The doctor smiled, held her near,
"Congrats, it's a girl, crystal-clear!"
Joy overflowed; my heart was light,
In that moment, pure delight.
A daughter's love, the world's best gift,
Her tiny face, my spirits lift.
Some may wish for boys instead,
But I have views of my own said.

A girl child's heart is strong and true,

A world of love in every hue.

She was born, my heart took flight,

A father's pride, both day and night.

For daughters stand through thick and thin,

In life's hard moments, they will win.

So, welcome girls with open arms,

See their strength, their love, and their charms.

Break the myths, let joy prevail,

For daughter's worth will never fail.

I'm proud of two, my joy and my light,

Fathers, cherish girls with all their might!"

Loving Life after Forty

At forty, life shifts, a turning tide,
No longer time to run or hide.
We feel the clock tick loud and clear,
A choice to change or stay right here.

It's time to pull up those big-girl pants,
Untie the strings, give life a chance.
Life after forty's fresh and bright,
A time to own your inner light.
Let go, release, embrace your grace,
And love your life with open space.

School Life and Real Life

Independent / Responsibilities

True Friends / Mean Friends

More Time / Limited Time

Fun / Worries

Unforgettable / Best Forgotten with Time

Exciting / Stressful

No Mind / Ego

Real Smile / Fake Smile.

The Internet's Hold

Hubby comes home, the day is done,
Children once rushed, now there's none.
The gates stay closed, no eager cheer,
A distant world has drawn them near.

He sinks into the couch's care,
TV remote held with a vacant stare.
Kids on games, their screens alight,
No family chatter to last the night.

The spouse arrives, her day a storm,
Switches channels, seeking form.
Daily soaps fill the air,
While hubby scrolls, with time to spare.

Working mom returns, worn and sore,
Children wait, their voices soar.

"Mama, Wi-Fi's slow again!"

"Take us out, let's go for ten!"

Crawling to the kitchen, tired and spent,

Her energy gone, her patience bent.

A call to hubby, quick and dry,

"Get dinner, please, I'm ready to cry."

Collapsing back, phone in hand,

The Wi-Fi world at her command.

School chats ping, college too,

Office texts, friends breaking through.

Group by group, the hours fade,

Till hubby's home, routine replayed.

In this webbed world, we've lost the thread,

Once vibrant homes feel dim instead.

Yet love and warmth still wait, we know,

If we put our screens down, let life glow.

Let the world outside begin to call,

And we rediscover life, one moment at a time, after all.

The Power of Smile

A smile can make love, a smile can make friends again,

A smile can bring into your life plenty of rain.

A smile can shed tears, a smile can remove fears,

A smile can bring all your loved ones near.

A smile can be fun, a smile can be fake,

A smile can awaken your life and make it great.

A smile is the best thing that Lord could make,

So friends keep smiling always for my sake.

The Jungle

Behind the walls of steel and glass,
lies a world both cruel and crass.
Where passion fades, where dreams are sold,
for power, greed, and lies untold.

The worker toils from dawn to night,
yet finds no fairness, sees no light.
His blood, his sweat, his silent pain,
All washed away like drops in rain.

The managers, perched on hollow thrones,
Feed on fear in measured tones.
They praise you now, they pull you near,
Then crush your soul and drown your cheer.

Politics dance in whispered breath,
A dagger cloaked in silk and death.
The cunning climb, the honest fall,
Integrity means nothing at all.

The rules are bent for chosen few,
While merit drowns in toxic dew.
Bias reigns, the strong survive,
But only those who scheme and thrive.

Yet through the smoke and shattered glass,
Some rise above, some will outlast.
For truth, though trampled, never dies,
It waits, it watches, then it flies.

So let them play their wicked game,
Let them chase their hollow fame.
For dignity, though bruised and torn,
Will rise anew with every morn.